# Building the
# New York Subway

**CORNERSTONES OF FREEDOM**™
**SECOND SERIES**

Andrew Santella

**Children's Press**®
A Division of Scholastic Inc.
New York • Toronto • London • Auckland • Sydney
Mexico City • New Delhi • Hong Kong
Danbury, Connecticut

Photographs © 2007: Alamy Images/Janine Wiedel Photolibrary: 41; Brown Brothers: 7, 10, 19, 26, 28, 29, 30, 45 bottom; Corbis Images: cover bottom, 5, 8, 18, 24, 25, 45 top (Bettmann), 27 (Underwood & Underwood); Getty Images: 34 (Mac Gramlich/Hulton Archive), 14 (Mansell/Time Life Pictures), 40 (Pix Inc./Time Life Pictures), 16, 44 bottom (Three Lions/Hulton Archive); Library of Congress/Underhill, NYC: 31; Mary Evans Picture Library: 11; New York Transit Museum: 3, 4, 20, 22, 32, 33, 36, 38; The Art Archive/Picture Desk/Culver Pictures: cover top, 12, 44 top.

Map by XNR Productions, Inc.


Library of Congress Cataloging-in-Publication Data
Santella, Andrew.
  Building the New York City subway / by Andrew Santella.
    p. cm. — (Cornerstones of freedom. Second series)
  ISBN-13: 978-0-516-23638-4
  ISBN-10: 0-516-23638-5
  1. Subways—New York (State)—New York—Design and construction—
Juvenile literature. I. Title. II. Series.
  TF847.N5S26 2007
  388.4'28097471—dc22                        2006006529

CHILDREN'S PRESS, CORNERSTONES OF FREEDOM™, and
associated logos are trademarks and/or registered trademarks of
Scholastic Library Publishing. SCHOLASTIC and associated logos
are trademarks and/or registered trademarks of Scholastic Inc.

1 2 3 4 5 6 7 8 9 10 R 16 15 14 13 12 11 10 09 08 07

NEW YORK CITY HAD BEEN waiting for this day for years. It was October 27, 1904, opening day of the city's brand-new subway. For decades, New Yorkers had talked of building a subway that would run below the busy streets and speed people around the growing city. Now that the subway was finally completed, New York City was celebrating.

Opening ceremonies for the subway were marked by patriotic decorations and crowds of New Yorkers looking forward to a ride.

All over the city, patriotic banners adorned buildings and church bells rang out. People lined up eagerly at the new subway stations to take their first rides.

No one was more thrilled than New York's mayor, George B. McClellan Jr. He had the honor of piloting the very first subway train on opening day. On board the train were the city's most powerful political and business leaders. Like the mayor, they were dressed for the special occasion in their finest clothes and top hats. The plan was for the mayor to drive the train a short distance, then hand over the controls to the train's real **motorman**.

But the mayor did not stick to the plan. He discovered that he enjoyed driving the train, and he stayed at the controls as he led it through station after station. He **accelerated** the train through the subway tunnel at 40 miles (64 kilometers) per hour—an incredible speed for New Yorkers used to the slow pace of horse-drawn **trolleys**. Along the train's route, subway workers and station guards lifted their hats and cheered as the train passed. But on board, subway officials were getting nervous. The last thing they wanted was an accident on the new subway's first day. One of them tried to remind the mayor to slow down. Another asked the mayor if he was ready to let the motorman take over.

City officials tour the City Hall subway station.

"I'm running this train!" the mayor answered defiantly.

Near what was then the Elm Street station, the train lurched to a sudden stop and passengers were sent tumbling out of their seats. The mayor, it seems, had accidentally hit the train's emergency brake. The dignitaries dusted themselves off and took their seats, and the train went on its way again. Eventually, a trained motorman took the controls and completed the journey without any further trouble. Once it was over, the mayor declared the first journey on the New York City subway a smashing success.

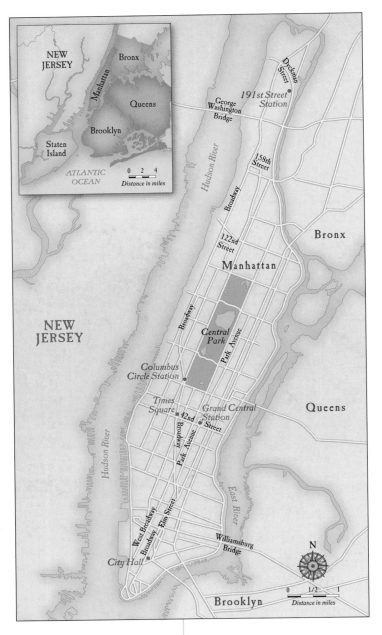

This map of Manhattan shows some of the major areas served by the subway. The city's five boroughs are shown in the inset.

Later that night, the gates of twenty-eight subway stations were thrown open, and more than 110,000 people got their first look at the new subway. They were delighted with what they saw. The subway was a wonder of engineering and technology. Out of solid rock and black earth, workers had cut an underground railway that could move New Yorkers around their city faster than ever. The subway made it easier for New Yorkers to get to their jobs and made it possible for them to move to new neighborhoods miles from the crowded center of the city. A British railway expert called the new subway "one of the great engineering achievements of the age." Life in New York City would never be the same again.

## THE BUSIEST CITY

In the last decades of the 1800s, New York was one of the busiest places in the world. Tens of thousands of **immigrants** from all over the world arrived in New York each year, and many settled in neighborhoods that were already overcrowded. By 1888, New York City had about four times as many residents as it did just sixty years earlier. New York City was taking in more new residents than it could handle.

Part of the problem was that New York's geography made it difficult to handle such rapid growth in population. The city sprawled across islands and other landmasses. It was split by rivers and bays. The heart of New York was Manhattan, a narrow island bordered by the East River and the Hudson River. Measuring just a few miles

## SETTLING NEW YORK

The first Europeans to settle New York were Dutch fur traders. They established a settlement called New Amsterdam in 1625. They and the English colonists who arrived later settled mostly along the southern end of Manhattan near New York Harbor. That area remained the most densely populated part of New York for centuries to come.

New York's growing population made getting around the city difficult.

7

In the 1800s, many New Yorkers depended on horse-drawn transportation.

across, Manhattan was home to New York's most crowded neighborhoods. On narrow streets lined with **tenements**, recent immigrants lived amid pollution and crime. Sometimes ten or more people shared a single small apartment. They had few other options for low-cost housing.

Just a few miles away, north of the city, open land waited to be turned into attractive new neighborhoods. But in the late 1800s, few working people could afford to move to these outlying areas. They would need a reliable and affordable way to travel from those areas to their jobs in the business districts of Manhattan. Without fast, reliable transportation, that open land would remain out of reach.

Meanwhile, transportation in New York City was a mess. Most streets were too crowded with traffic and too noisy for conversation. Horse-drawn carriages, trolleys, and pedestrians battled for space. Without any traffic signals, street corners often turned into scenes of chaos. Getting from one place to another usually took an extraordinary amount of time. Mark Twain wrote of having taken more than four hours to travel 3 miles (5 km) on a New York City street. Another writer gave this advice for crossing a New York street: "Look up street and down street, and see what carts and carriages are upon you, and then run for your life."

New Yorkers in the late 1800s could choose from a wide range of transportation options, but they were all too slow and too crowded. Some parts of the city were served by horse-drawn railroads. The railroad cars were simple wooden boxes on four wheels that were pulled by teams of two horses. The trains ran on iron rails in the surface of the street, and passengers rode inside the trains and on the roofs. Another option was the omnibus, a horse-drawn wagon that could carry twelve to fifteen passengers.

The fastest means of transportation was the elevated train. El trains, as they were called, began running in New York in 1867. They traveled on tracks laid atop iron girders high above the city's streets. With 94 miles (151 km) of tracks, the El served much of Manhattan. Brooklyn also had a network of elevated lines. The trains moved at a rate of about 12 miles (19 km) per hour, which was considered speedy. But they generated thick black smoke, and many people complained that the trains were too loud and too dirty. Pedestrians who walked under the tracks might find themselves dodging falling **cinders** and oil dripping from the trains. The El was not the answer to New York City's transportation problems.

**Elevated trains were fast, but also noisy and smoky.**

## SUBWAY DREAMS

What New York needed was a high-speed transportation system that could carry large numbers of passengers. People began proposing a subway for New York as early as the 1840s. In the 1860s, a railroad executive from Michigan

named Hugh B. Willson promised that he could build a
Manhattan subway that would offer a fast and comfortable
ride. "The passenger would be sure of a luxurious seat in a
well-lighted car, and would be carried to his destination in
one-third the time he could be carried by any other convey-
ance," Willson wrote. Best of all, he added, there would be
"no dust . . . no mud."

But plans for building a subway in New York were
always stalled by local politics. In New York City, much
of the political power lay in the hands of William Marcy

New York City offered
many transit choices,
but none met the needs
of the growing city.

**William Marcy "Boss" Tweed**

"Boss" Tweed. As commissioner of public works, he collected fees from the operators of streetcars, omnibuses, and other public transportation systems. The money he collected helped him gather and maintain political power. Tweed feared that a new subway would put other transportation systems out of business and deprive him of his source of funds. So he made sure that plans for a subway in New York went nowhere.

# INNOVATION—AND A SECRET

Tweed's corrupt politics did not discourage one inventor. As early as 1849, twenty-three-year-old Alfred Ely Beach had proposed building a subway under Broadway in New York to help solve traffic problems on that busy street. Beach's first plans involved using horses to pull trains in the tunnel. Later, however, he began working on plans to use compressed air to push the trains through the tunnels. He knew that cities such as London used compressed air tunnels to move mail and small packages across town. Beach's plan was to adapt the idea to move people, too. He invented a system that used huge fans to create enough air pressure to drive entire subway trains.

In 1867, at an industrial fair in New York, Beach unveiled a small version of his proposed subway tunnel. The tube he constructed was just 100 feet (30 meters) long, but it held a train car that could carry ten people inside. Thousands of people flocked to the fair to experience riding in an air-propelled train, and Beach's invention became the talk of New York. But his plans got little support from local government officials.

So Beach came up with a way to get around the opposition of Boss Tweed. He refused to pay **bribes** to Tweed and other corrupt politicians to get his subway built. Instead, he planned to build secretly a block-long subway beneath the city streets to demonstrate once and for all that his system would work. He hoped that when he opened the subway to the public, the response would be so favorable that local officials would have no choice but to support it.

**LONDON'S SUBWAY**

The world's first subway was London's Metropolitan Railway, which opened in 1863. Equipped with steam locomotives designed for use in underground tunnels, the subway was a huge success. It later became part of London's Underground, an extensive system also known as the tube.

13

**This photograph, taken in 1912, shows the remains of Beach's first subway train, found underneath Murray Street.**

Beach resolved to build a subway without revealing his secret. Most amazing of all, he did it almost right under the noses of City Hall politicians. He rented a vacant clothing store near City Hall, hired a crew of workers, and began digging a tunnel beneath Broadway. The tunnel stretched for one city block, between Murray and Warren streets. To maintain secrecy, Beach's crew worked only at night. Eight feet (2.4 m) wide and 12 feet (3.7 m) below street level, the tunnel was a terrible workplace. Hot, dark, smelly, and filled with the sound of horses clattering on the street above, the tunnel tested the courage of the workers.

Beach invented tunneling equipment to assist the project's completion. One of his inventions was a digging machine called a pneumatic shield that helped Beach's crew finish the tunnel in just fifty-eight nights. When it was completed, the tunnel was 312 feet (95 m) long.

Beach's key piece of machinery was a huge fan called the Roots Patent Force Blast blower, or the Western Tornado. It weighed 50 tons, and Beach assembled the enormous fan at one end of his secret subway tunnel. When turned on, it produced a blast of air so massive that it could push a subway train at about 10 miles (16 km) per hour. When the air power had pushed the train all the way to the far end of the tunnel, the fan could be reversed so that it would suck the train back to its starting point. Incredible as it sounds, Beach's system worked.

**ALFRED ELY BEACH**

The subway was hardly Alfred Ely Beach's only interest. He also developed inventions such as a typewriter for blind people. When he wasn't working on his inventions, Beach kept busy as the editor and co-owner of *Scientific American* magazine. Under his leadership, the magazine became one of the most famous technical publications in the world. It is still published today.

**Passengers wait to board Beach's pneumatic subway.**

## A SUBWAY REVEALED

By February 26, 1870, Beach was ready to unveil his secret subway. It became an instant sensation, attracting tens of thousands of visitors. Even before they saw the subway in action, they were impressed with the station Beach had built. It was decorated with chandeliers, a grandfather clock, a grand piano, and a fountain stocked with goldfish.

Clean and well-lit, the station helped reassure people who were nervous about journeying belowground.

Curious New Yorkers paid twenty-five cents each to ride on Beach's block-long subway. Each car held twenty-two people, and many came away convinced that Beach's invention could help solve New York's transportation problems. In fact, Beach proposed building a bigger subway—one that would run 5 miles (8 km), from City Hall to Central Park.

But that subway would never be built. Although Beach's system worked, it had serious drawbacks. It was difficult to control the speed of the trains, which was an important consideration in a large subway system. Nor would it be easy to run many trains at once on one subway line. Beach's biggest problem was securing the political and financial backing for the subway. A stock market panic in 1873 ended any hope of finding money to build his underground railway. Beach's idea was soon forgotten, and his secretly constructed tunnel was closed.

In the end, it took a natural disaster to convince New Yorkers to build a subway. In March 1888, a blizzard dumped snow on New York City for two days, and winds of 50 miles (80 km) per hour created drifts 25 feet (7.6 m) high. The storm completely shut down public transportation in the city. El trains became stuck in mountains of snow.

**BEACH'S SUBWAY**

Alfred Ely Beach's experimental subway lay buried for more than forty years. Then in 1912, a work crew was digging a new subway tunnel for the Brooklyn Rapid Transit Company. The crew broke through an old brick wall beneath the city's streets and came upon Beach's subway tunnel. Inside they discovered the remains of his subway train, his waiting room, and some of the digging equipment he invented. Beach's old tunnel was incorporated into the newer and larger subway.

The blizzard of 1888 shut down transportation in New York City.

Omnibuses were abandoned in the streets. New Yorkers were unable to get to their jobs, and many could not even get to stores to buy milk or bread. Some people froze to death in the streets. The city stopped working.

## MAYOR HEWITT'S PLAN

The blizzard demonstrated how much New Yorkers relied on public transportation. Even before the blizzard struck, Mayor Abram S. Hewitt had been pushing for a new public transportation system. Unlike some other city leaders,

Hewitt believed that public transportation was essential to the city and that it was the city government's responsibility to provide reliable transportation. He began talking of building an urban railway that would send trains rushing across town at 40 miles (64 km) per hour. To commuters who were used to slow trips of 5 miles (8 km) per hour on horse-drawn railroads, this sounded incredible. Hewitt appealed to New Yorkers' pride by pointing out that other cities, including Boston, were busy building subways. Didn't New York deserve the best and most modern transportation system? To Hewitt, that meant building a subway.

Not everyone agreed. To some people, the whole idea of going underground to ride in trains sounded absurd and unsafe. Some local political leaders argued that the city had no business building railways. But Hewitt had a unique plan for public transportation, and slowly he won the support of civic and business leaders. His idea was for city government and private business to work together. The city would own the subway and finance its construction; a private railroad company would build and manage it.

New York mayor Abram S. Hewitt supported building a subway.

Hewitt's plan won the support of New Yorkers. In a **referendum** held in 1894, voters approved the idea of using city funds to build a public transit system. To turn the plan into reality, the Board of Rapid Transit Railroad Commissioners (RTC) was formed. One of the RTC's first tasks was getting the legal permission to construct subway tunnels underneath New York. The RTC had to battle property owners who were worried that subway construction would damage the foundations of their buildings. Merchants feared that aboveground subway construction sites would keep customers from reaching their stores and businesses. But after years of negotiations, the RTC won the right to build tunnels under New York.

**August Belmont**

In 1899, the RTC began accepting bids, or offers, to build and operate the subway. In 1900, a wealthy businessman named August Belmont was awarded the contract to "build, equip, and operate the railroad for fifty years." The city agreed to provide him with $36.5 million to cover construction costs and land purchases. Once the subway was finished, Belmont would collect passenger fees and begin paying back the city for the building costs.

Belmont had made his money in banking and had little experience in transportation. But he hoped building New York's subway would make him a local hero and earn him another fortune. He believed he could make "a great deal of money out of schemes for improving the transportation in our large and growing cities." As it turned out, Belmont did make another fortune from the subway. But the job was such a difficult one that he often wondered why he had ever become involved in it.

## WILLIAM BARCLAY PARSONS AND THE IRT

August Belmont formed a new company called the Interborough Rapid Transit Company (IRT). The job of directing construction belonged to an engineer named William Barclay Parsons. An experienced railroad man, Parsons had worked on huge public works projects such as the Panama Canal. However, he had never tackled a project quite like the New York City subway. "Had I fully realized all that was ahead of me," Parsons later wrote, "I do not think I could have attempted the work."

Parsons took on the subway job with such passion that it almost took over his life. He personally oversaw all aspects of building and planning the subway. To work out the best possible route for the subway, he walked mile

**NEW YORK'S BOROUGHS**

New York City is divided into five areas called boroughs: the Bronx, Brooklyn, Manhattan, Queens, and Staten Island. Today's subway system serves all the boroughs except remote Staten Island, located across the Verrazano Narrows from Brooklyn.

**William Barclay Parsons**

★ ★ ★ ★

after mile through the streets of Manhattan. And he convinced the best engineers in the business to come to New York to work for him.

The path that Parsons laid out for the subway would run almost 24 miles (37 km). The lines tunneled through **bedrock**, ran under riverbeds, and crossed one deep valley on elevated steel tracks. Starting at City Hall in lower Manhattan, passengers would be able to ride north to 42nd Street. There they could connect with above ground railroad lines at Grand Central Station, New York's huge railroad depot. The subway then headed west to the new Times Square, then north again to the upper reaches of Manhattan.

At 122nd Street, subway trains would emerge from underground. This was the beginning of a dip in the landscape called the Manhattan Valley, and Parsons decided that the best way to cross the valley was on elevated tracks. So he designed a steel-arch **viaduct** that would carry the subway trains high aboveground for twelve blocks. Back underground, the subway crossed into the Bronx and ended amid farmland. Subway planners hoped that new **suburbs** would spring up along the subway's northern reaches, providing much-needed housing for New Yorkers.

One of the first decisions Parsons had to make was how to power his subway trains. He traveled around the world to examine and learn from other subway systems. As he traveled, he became more and more interested in using electricity to drive trains. In the last several decades, the world had entered an electric age, using electricity to power streetlights, motors, and many new inventions. Engineers had begun using it in railroads and subways, too. Part of London's underground railway ran on electricity, and in many ways it ran more smoothly than the old steam-powered sections. Paris was planning to build its own electric subway. Prague (now in the Czech Republic) and Budapest (now in Hungary) already had electric-powered subways. Much closer to home, so did Boston.

Compared to steam and coal power, electricity offered a much cleaner ride. Electricity helped spare passengers from choking on smelly fumes and having their clothes ruined by **soot**. But what railroad companies really liked about electricity was that it saved them money. Electric power was less expensive than other forms of power. It also required fewer workers, so companies saved money on labor, too. Not surprisingly, Parsons chose to power his subway with electricity.

After years of debate, New York City was ready to build its subway. On March 24, 1900, New York City celebrated the start of construction with fireworks, church bells, and a display of thousands of American flags. Some 25,000 people gathered in a park across from City Hall to mark the occasion.

## BUILDING THE IRT

Before it was completed, some 77,000 workers would help build the subway. Miners came from across the United States to dig the deepest tunnels. Bricklayers and carpenters built subway stops and **powerhouses**. And whole

**Parsons knew that an electric-powered subway such as Boston's (shown here under construction) would be cleaner and less expensive than other forms of transportation.**

Construction of the subway left huge holes in New York streets.

armies of workers called muckers moved the mountains of dirt displaced by the digging. Sometimes workers uncovered buried treasure. Digging the tunnels, they came upon old tools and weapons from New York's distant past. Work crews turned up the remains of a Dutch ship named the *Tiger*, a **relic** of New York's days as a Dutch colony. Near Dyckman Street, workers found something older still: bones from a prehistoric **mastodon**.

But mostly they found danger and hard work. There were hundreds of accidents, explosions, cave-ins, and other mishaps. Thousands of workers were injured building the subway, and at least forty-four workers and civilians lost their lives in construction accidents.

The work was done almost entirely by hand. Diggers used some modern-style heavy equipment, but much of the tunneling was done with shovels, picks, and muscle. Load after load of dirt was dumped into wheelbarrows, then into horse-drawn carts. The carts were driven to empty fields at the edge of the city and dumped. When diggers encountered hard rock, their shovels and picks were of little use. They used dynamite to blast away at the rock and form their tunnels. Not surprisingly, the use of explosives resulted in more accidents, injuries, and deaths.

**Working conditions beneath the streets were dangerous and difficult.**

This cave-in occurred at Broadway and 38th Street. The taxi in the foreground fell in when the street sank, but was hoisted out.

New York's landscape held many surprises for subway workers and posed real danger. They had to contend with hills, valleys, plains, and rocky bluffs. They encountered underground rivers and ponds, and had to work around quicksand and solid rock. Much of Manhattan was covered in schist, a hard but unstable rock. Some schist is so hard and dense that it is difficult to cut through. But it can also be crumbly and brittle, making it unpredictable and dangerous to work with.

Some early subways were built deep underground in tunnels dug out of bedrock. But in New York City, the location of the bedrock varied from place to place. In some areas, bedrock ran only 10 feet (3 m) below the streets. In other areas, the bedrock was as much as 50 feet (15 m) deep. Parsons decided not to dig his tunnels out of bedrock at all. Instead, he would set the tunnels close to the surface—just about 15 feet (4.5 m) below the streets of the city.

The city's varied landscape posed many challenges for the subway builders to overcome.

To create most of the subway, workers used a method called "cut and cover." First, workers dug a trench out of the street, usually about 50 feet (15 m) wide. Then they built a steel frame along the walls of the trench. On the bottom of the trench, they laid a concrete floor and four sets of railroad tracks—two each for trains going in either direction. A cement wall was built to separate the two sets of tracks, and guardrails were installed. When the tracks were complete and a steel-and-concrete roof was in place, workers covered up the top of the trench. The result was an underground tube that could hold four subway trains at once.

The cut-and-cover method was easier and less expensive than tunneling deep underground. It had been used successfully on other subways, including the one in Budapest. But it posed some problems for New York City work crews. They had to work amid a tangle of sewer lines, water pipes, **gas mains**, and other man-made obstacles just beneath the streets. Plumbing and telephone lines had to be relocated. Crews had to work around building foundations, taking care not to damage them.

The cut-and-cover method involved digging a shallow trench in city streets.

Not all of New York City's subway was built using the cut-and-cover method. Sometimes the city's **terrain** forced workers to use other methods. In some places, trains ran on elevated tracks instead of underground. In other places, crews had to resort to digging deep tunnels through rock. They dug deep shafts down from the street until they hit rock. Then they drilled holes into the rock and filled the holes with dynamite. After setting off the dynamite (from a safe distance), workers crawled back down the shaft to clear away the rubble. They built frames to hold up rock and earth, then planted more dynamite. The process was repeated, with explosion after explosion, until a tunnel had been cleared.

New Yorkers learned to live with the noise and dust of the dynamite blasts. Bottles rattled on store shelves, and houses shook. And when workers made mistakes, the results were awful. One dynamite explosion caused an entire block of Park Avenue to cave in.

The deepest rock tunnel began north of 158th Street and extended to the 191st Street station. At 180 feet (290 m) belowground, the tunnel was so deep that workers had to install an elevator for passengers to reach stations. (The

Subway workers cut through rock with a steam-powered drill.

The sights and sounds of construction work became commonplace to New Yorkers.

## LIGHTING THE TUNNELS

A number of different methods were used to light up the dark subway tunnels. Where tunnels were close enough to the surface, glass **skylights** were built into the ceilings to let in daylight. Walls of stations were often lined with light-colored tiles to better reflect light. And throughout the subway, electric lights ran along the walls to illuminate the tunnels.

191st Street station is still the deepest in the New York City subway system.) Miners from the western United States came to New York to work on the tunnel, which they called the mine. In 1903, crews were blasting away at the tunnel, under pressure from their bosses to work quickly. Suddenly, an explosion caused a collapse inside the tunnel, and a 300-ton boulder fell, killing several miners instantly. In all, ten workers lost their lives in the accident.

There were other terrible accidents. In January 1902, a shed full of dynamite exploded and destroyed a nearby hotel and several other buildings. Five people were killed

in the blast. Later that year, an accident claimed the life of a supervisor named Ira Shaler. Shaler had been touring the tunnels with William Barclay Parsons when Parsons mentioned that a section of the roof looked a little weak. Shaler told Parsons the roof was "perfectly safe," but just then the roof caved in. Shaler was buried in rock and was killed. Parsons did not suffer a scratch.

Despite the accidents, work continued. New Yorkers became accustomed to seeing construction equipment all over the streets. Some streets disappeared completely, torn up in the cut-and-cover process. But the noise of digging, blasting, and building told people that construction was moving forward. As the subway neared completion, only one question remained: Would New Yorkers accept the subway?

## THE SUBWAY BEGINS ITS RUN

The answer became clear on October 27, 1904. That day, the subway was opened to the people of New York City, and they loved what they saw. More than 100,000 people

Subway company officials perform a safety inspection prior to the subway's opening.

swarmed through the gates to explore the new subway. Extra police officers had to be called in to control the crowds. Passengers were impressed with the stations, which were decorated with handsome tile **mosaics** and graceful arches.

The grandest station served City Hall in lower Manhattan. It boasted stained-glass skylights, domed ceilings, and decorative brick and stone details. Many stations featured artwork related to the name of the station. For example, the walls of Columbus Circle station showed images of one of Christopher Columbus's ships.

The most impressive thing about the subway, though, was its speed. Express trains on the IRT traveled at more

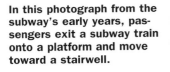

In this photograph from the subway's early years, passengers exit a subway train onto a platform and move toward a stairwell.

*  *  *  *

than 40 miles (64 km) per hour. Riders were delighted to be able to cross from one end of the city to another in a fraction of the time it used to take. The speed of the subway made distant neighborhoods more attractive places to live. Builders developed homes and apartment buildings in areas that had once been farmland. New suburbs and new neighborhoods began to spring up around the edges of New York City. The population of the Bronx and northern Manhattan rose rapidly.

By 1908, more than 800,000 passengers were riding the New York subway each day. The city experienced another new reality: the rush-hour crush on the subway. Passengers waited in long lines and squeezed into crowded cars. It soon became obvious New York City could use even more subways. "There is not a street in the city that cannot be tunneled," one subway planner said.

But who would build the new subways? Belmont wanted all the subway business in New York for himself. But some business and civic leaders didn't like the idea of one person holding so much power. They believed that healthy business competition would result in better subway service for New York. So in 1913, the city decided to work with two subway companies: Belmont's IRT and a new company called the Brooklyn Rapid Transit Company (BRT). The two companies would build new subways that would connect Manhattan with Brooklyn. The new lines would double the

**STRAPHANGERS**

From the beginning, New York City subway cars featured strap loops hanging from the ceiling for standing passengers to hold on to. They helped passengers keep their balance during the lurching ride. Subway riders are still sometimes called straphangers.

August Belmont's subway car, the *Mineola*, featured carpeting, oval windows, and a roll-top desk.

## THE *MINEOLA*

August Belmont liked to ride the subway, but he rode in grand style. He had his own subway car, the *Mineola*. It featured plush seats, bathrooms, and even a dining table.

size of the subway system, with hundreds of miles of new track. And they would help unite the boroughs of New York City. Because the city signed contracts to work with two rival companies at once, the arrangement was called the Dual Service contracts system.

The new subway expansion called for eight new tunnels that would run beneath New York City's waterways. These underwater tunnels posed special challenges and dangers for work crews. Crews worked under the constant risk of cave-ins and floods. If there was one crack in the tunnel wall, tons of water would come crashing through, flooding the tunnel. The crews working on underwater tunnels called themselves sandhogs, and they took special pride in doing the most dangerous work.

Construction on the new lines was completed in the early 1920s, and New York was able to claim the largest subway in the world. The expanded subway system reached into areas of Brooklyn, Queens, and Manhattan that had never been adequately served by mass transit before. Once again, the new subway lines helped spur the building of new housing and new communities in outlying areas.

## TROUBLE IN THE SUBWAYS

But the new subway system was far from perfect. One source of trouble was the ongoing competition between the IRT and the BRT. Each company refused to cooperate with the other. As a result, the BRT's larger subway cars could not fit in the smaller IRT tunnels. In addition, New York's fascination with subways was ending. Automobiles were becoming more common, offering more convenient transportation for many. By 1917, New York City mayor John Hylan was regularly criticizing the IRT and BRT for cheating their passengers and providing poor service.

Then on November 18, 1918, a disaster shook the public's confidence in the subways. A subway train running at 60 miles (97 km) per hour jumped its tracks and slammed into a concrete tunnel wall near Malbone Street. The accident killed ninety-three passengers, and the mayor accused the BRT of "reckless disregard for human life." With its reputation damaged, the BRT folded in 1923. It was replaced by the Brooklyn-Manhattan Transit Company, or BMT.

Still, New York City was not finished building its subway. In 1925, the city formed yet another company to build new lines. The Independent Subway system (IND) was owned and operated by the city. It launched a third phase of subway construction, adding twenty-eight new stations and 190 miles (306 km) of track. These new lines ran mostly through areas that were already developed, instead of reaching out

**The wreck of the Malbone Street subway, which crashed on November 18, 1918**

toward new suburbs. They helped make traveling more convenient for commuters and provided more ways for travelers to reach their destinations.

Construction methods had advanced so far by the time the IND lines were built that the subway expansion was completed without any major explosions, accidents, or tunnel cave-ins. Yet New Yorkers found little reason to be excited by the new subway lines. By the 1930s, subways no longer seemed modern and thrilling. With automobile and airplane traffic becoming more common, people took speedy transportation for granted. The last major subway construction project in New York City was completed in 1940.

By then, the entire subway system had become the property of New York City. In 1939, the city had purchased the IRT and BMT systems for $326 million. Built by a series of companies over nearly forty years, the New York City subway system was finally unified under the ownership of the city itself. It was the biggest transit system in the world. More than a million passengers rode the subway in its first year under city ownership. It employed some 35,000 conductors, motormen, security guards, and other workers.

New York celebrated the city's unification of the subway system on June 1, 1940. Mayor Fiorello H. La Guardia put on a motorman's cap and uniform jacket and posed for photographers aboard a subway train. Unlike Mayor McClellan thirty-six years earlier, he did not try to drive the train. He left the driving to the real motormen.

Mayor Fiorello La Guardia, aboard a subway car, celebrates the city's unified subway system.

## TODAY'S SUBWAY

New Yorkers still depend on the subway to get around. For many, it is hard to imagine daily life without it. The subway carries passengers to work, to school, to stores, to major league baseball games, to movie theaters, to Broadway shows, and just about anywhere they want to go in New York City. It is the longest transportation system in the world, with more than 700 miles (1,127 km) of track. Some 2.7 million residents and visitors ride the subway every day, making it one of the busiest transit systems in the world.

Built over four decades, the subway was a massive construction project that overcame dangerous natural obstacles. To many, building the subway seemed foolish or impossible. But the subway succeeded in changing life in New York City.

The subway is a part of daily life for many New Yorkers.

# Glossary

**accelerated**—drove with increased speed

**bedrock**—the solid layer of rock under the soil and loose rock

**bribes**—dishonest payments made in return for favorable treatment

**cinders**—small pieces of wood or coal that have been partly burned

**gas mains**—underground pipes that deliver gas to homes and businesses

**immigrants**—people who have come from one country to live permanently in another

**mastodon**—an extinct mammal resembling an elephant

**mosaics**—patterns or pictures made up of small pieces of colored stone, tile, or glass

**motorman**—the operator or driver of a subway train

**powerhouses**—stations that generate electricity

**referendum**—a vote taken to determine whether a proposed law should be passed

**relic**—something left behind from the distant past

**skylights**—windows cut into ceilings to allow natural light to enter a place

**soot**—black powder produced when a fuel such as coal, wood, or oil burns

**suburbs**—areas or districts on or close to the outer edge of a city; suburbs are made up mostly of homes, with few businesses

**tenements**—rundown apartment buildings that are crowded and in a poor part of a city

**terrain**—ground or land

**trolleys**—streetcars that run on tracks set in a city street

**viaduct**—a large bridge that carries a railroad track, road, or pipeline across a valley or over a city street

# Timeline: Building the

| 1849 | 1870 | 1899 | 1900 | 1904 |
|------|------|------|------|------|
| Alfred Ely Beach proposes building a small subway in New York. | Beach unveils his secretly built air-powered subway. | New York's Board of Rapid Transit Railroad Commissioners takes bids for construction of the city's first large-scale subway. | MARCH 24 Construction begins on the Interborough Rapid Transit Company subway. | OCTOBER 27 Mayor George B. McClellan Jr. presides at the opening of the IRT subway. |

# New York Subway

## 1908

The subway attracts 800,000 riders each day.

## 1913

New York City issues Dual Service contracts to Interborough Rapid Transit Company and Brooklyn Rapid Transit Company.

## 1925

New York City mayor John Hylan announces plan for a city-owned and operated system called the IND; ground is broken for the first IND subway line.

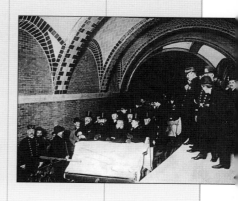

## 1932

The IND line is opened and dedicated.

## 1939

BMT and IRT become property of the City of New York for $326 million.

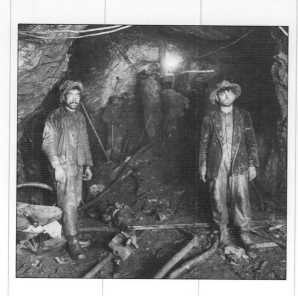

# To Find Out More

## BOOKS

Brimner, Larry Dane. *Subway: The Story of Tunnels, Tubes, and Tracks.* Honesdale, Pa.: Boyds Mills Press, 2004.

Fischler, Stan. *Subways of the World.* Osceola, Wis.: Motorbooks International, 2000.

McGovern, Ann. . . . *If You Lived 100 Years Ago.* New York: Scholastic Paperbacks, 2000.

Weitzman, David. *A Subway for New York.* New York: Farrar, Straus & Giroux, 2005.

## ONLINE SITES

New York Transit Museum
*http://www.mta.info/mta/museum*

NYC Subway
*http://www.nycsubway.org*

# Index

Bold numbers indicate illustrations.

# About the Author

**Andrew Santella** is the author of numerous nonfiction books for children and has written for the *New York Times Book Review*, *GQ*, and other publications. He lives with his wife and son in northern Illinois.